# THE VICTORIANS
## RECONSTRUCTED

Liz Gogerly

Photographs by Martyn F. Chillmaid

HODDER
Wayland

An imprint of Hodder Children's Books

# RECONSTRUCTED

Other titles in this series:
**The Home Front • The Romans
The Saxons and Vikings • The Tudors • The Victorians**

Conceived and produced for Hodder Wayland by

**Nutshell**
MEDIA

Intergen House, 65–67 Western Road, Hove BN3 2JQ, UK
www.nutshellmedialtd.co.uk

© Copyright 2003 Nutshell Media

Editor: Polly Goodman
Designer: Simon Borrough
All reconstructions set-up and photographed by: Martyn F. Chillmaid
Photograph page 27: Alvey & Towers

First published in Great Britain in 2003 by Hodder Wayland,
an imprint of Hodder Children's Books.

Reprinted in 2003

British Library Cataloguing in Publication Data
Gogerly, Liz
The Victorians. – (Reconstructed)
1. Great Britain – Social life and customs – 19th century – Pictorial works – Juvenile literature
2. Great Britain – History – Victoria, 1837–1901 – Pictorial works – Juvenile literature
I. Title
941'.081'0222

ISBN 0 7502 4313 9

Printed and bound in China

Hodder Children's Books
A division of Hodder Headline Limited
338 Euston Road, London NW1 3BH

Cover photographs: main photo: two child miners push a wagon out of a pit; from top to
bottom: a Victorian street scene; a printer checks that a poster has printed properly; a boatman
legs his narrowboat through a tunnel; a butcher's shop; a chemist making pills.

Title page: A typical Victorian street scene.

# Contents

# Who Were the Victorians?

**A middle-class Victorian family dressed in their best clothes pose for a family portrait.**

The Victorian era began in 1837 when Queen Victoria came to the throne. Victoria was just 18 years old when she became queen, and her reign would last until she died in 1901, aged 81. In 1840 Victoria married her German cousin, Albert, and over the next 17 years they had nine children together. The royal family was hugely popular and their happy family life became a role model for most families at the time. In 1861, the royal family was photographed together in one of the first ever portrait photographs. Soon after, many middle-class families had their photographs taken too.

Sailor suit

Satin and lace gown

Best hat

Lace frills

Cotton and lace shirt

Waistcoat, jacket and tie

By the mid-nineteenth century, there were millions of middle-class families living in Britain's industrial towns and cities. The father of each family had a respectable job such as a lawyer or banker. He worked hard to support his family, but in return he demanded obedience from his wife and children.

Most Victorian children knew the saying that 'children should be seen and not heard'. They had many rules to obey, such as keeping silent at the dinner table and not speaking unless they were spoken to. If they disobeyed, they risked being beaten with a leather strap.

In Victorian times there was no birth control, so many families had as many as ten children. Poorer families were usually crammed into small, overcrowded houses. Older children were expected to help their mothers run the home and look after their younger brothers and sisters. Children as young as 8 often had to work rather than go to school, to help provide for their family. It wasn't until 1870 that it became the law that all children aged between 5 and 13 had to go to school. Life for more wealthy children wasn't always easy either. They were usually raised by a nanny in the nursery and rarely saw their parents.

A girl with her *Girl's Own* annual, wearing clothes typical of the late nineteenth century.

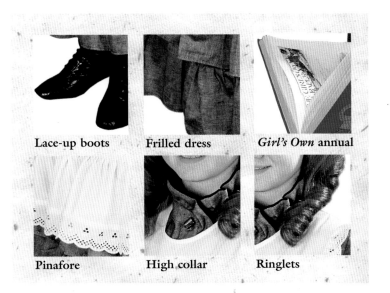

Lace-up boots    Frilled dress    *Girl's Own* annual

Pinafore    High collar    Ringlets

# The Industrial Revolution

**A miner arrives at the pit early in the morning.**

By the beginning of Queen Victoria's reign, Britain was known as 'the workshop of the world'. Large deposits of coal, iron, copper and tin provided the raw materials for industry, and Britain led the way in the industrial revolution. The country became the world's leading supplier of iron and steel, and its manufacturing industry was the envy of the world.

Coal was important to Britain's success because it was used to make steam, which powered factories and later, locomotives. Most industrial centres sprang up next to coalfields in northern England, Scotland and south Wales. Mining was back-breaking work, yet when demand for coal soared, children as young as 4 were often employed in the pits. Sometimes miners had to crawl along tunnels just 75 centimetres high. They faced hazards such as poison gas, and suffered bronchitis and asthma from the coal dust.

Miner

Site office

Coal

Pithead winding gear

In Victorian times, the only way of exporting or importing goods from abroad was by ship. At the end of the eighteenth century, the fastest way of transporting goods over long distances was on wooden sailing ships, called clippers. They carried tea and spices from Asia to England, and manufactured goods to North America.

At the beginning of the nineteenth century, new technology was transforming the shipbuilding industry and the first steamships started to replace sailing ships. These ships needed a lot of coal on board and had to make stops to refuel. The race was on to design ships that would be strong enough to carry more coal, so they would not have to stop and refuel and the journeys would become shorter. Once more Britain led the way and in 1843 the engineer Isambard Kingdom Brunel designed and built the *Great Britain*, the first steamship made of iron.

Rope       Oakum

Barrel of tar       Wooden boat

**Two boatyard workers roll oakum into rope. It will be knocked into the seams of wooden boats and covered in tar to make them watertight.**

# The Changing Workplace

During Victoria's reign, people flocked to the industrial towns and cities from the countryside in search of employment in factories, textile mills and mines. By 1881, it is estimated that over a third of Britain's working population was employed in manufacturing.

Apart from factory workers and miners, there was still a growing number of traditional craftsmen, such as carpenters, blacksmiths, shoemakers and tailors. Craftsmen like these had to complete seven-year apprenticeships before they became fully qualified.

Like everyone else in Victorian times, the craftsman's work was made easier by the new technologies that were being developed at the time. In the 1850s, a new type of sewing machine meant that shoemakers could work more quickly and make more shoes. From the 1870s, factory-made shoes also became available. The shoemaker was still kept in business though, making handmade shoes for his more well-off, or 'well-heeled' customers.

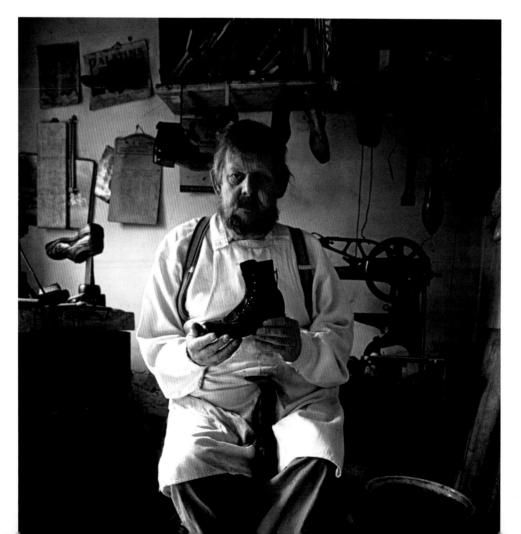

A shoemaker in his workshop.

Lace-up boot

Shoe last (mould)

Sewing machine

**A printer checks that a poster has printed properly.**

The Victorians invented machines for every kind of process imaginable. Some of these machines could be powered by steam, but many also relied on people. The first steam printing presses were being used in England in the early 1800s. The press was powered by steam, but the printer still had to select the individual wooden letters required.

Printer · Poster

Steam printing press · Wooden letter blocks

In the Victorian era, one new invention usually led to other exciting developments. For example in the nineteenth century, new advances in printing technology made it possible to print on both sides of a sheet of paper. Soon it was possible to print on rolls of paper rather than sheets. In turn, this meant that newspapers could be mass-produced and sold to many more people.

In 1851, Britain showed off its manufacturing achievements in the Great Exhibition, the world's first industrial fair. It was held in the Crystal Palace, a revolutionary building built out of glass and iron, in London.

# Child Labour

Children were an important part of the Victorian workforce, but they were also the most badly treated. They provided cheap labour and because they were young, they were easy to boss about. In early Victorian times some children worked from five in the morning until nine o'clock at night. In the mines, children were employed to open doors or pick among the rubble to find pieces of coal. Children were also employed in factories. Their fast little fingers were perfect for working the machinery and their tiny bodies meant that they could crawl under moving machinery to clean it.

**Two boys struggle with a wagon filled with coal.**

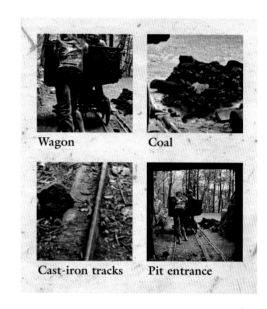

Wagon    Coal

Cast-iron tracks    Pit entrance

Industrial towns attracted large numbers of single workers, which led to many unwanted children being born. These children were put in institutions such as workhouses, apprentice houses and hospitals for foundlings. Apprentice houses were run by owners of cotton mills and other factories. Children served apprenticeships in their factories for seven years, and in return they were fed, clothed, housed and schooled. Child apprentices would have known only discipline and hard work. Wardens supervised their every move and when they weren't working in the factory, they had lessons or tended the garden and mended clothes. Even so, they would have counted themselves lucky not to be in the workhouse.

Social campaigners like Anthony Ashley, the 7th Earl of Shaftesbury, fought to change the laws regarding child labour. In 1833, the first of a series of new laws meant that children under the age of nine were not to be employed in factories. Later, this age limit was raised and the working day was cut to ten hours. However, the new laws didn't help the thousands of children who worked in illegal sweat shops, or slaved on farms. In the 1870s, it became law for all children aged between 5 and 13 to go to school, but poverty and family hardship meant many children carried on working after school hours.

**The dormitory of this apprentice house would have seemed luxurious compared to the workhouse.**

Wooden bed

Woollen blanket

Chamber pot

Candle lamp

Broom

Laundry basket

# Life in the Countryside

A woman feeds her pigs with kitchen waste to fatten them up before killing them.

Sty

Bucket of feed

Vegetable patch

Squatters' cottage

For those families left in the Victorian countryside, life was tough. In the late eighteenth and early nineteenth century, rich landowners had taken over common land to use for commercial farming. People who had worked on the land for centuries suddenly had to rent the land off landowners, or work as labourers on their farms. The industrial revolution brought more hardship to farm labourers because steam-powered machinery replaced many of their jobs. Cheap imports of grain from America meant that many farmers turned to livestock farming instead. Farm labourers had to survive on smaller and smaller wages.

Poor families living in the countryside relied on animals and vegetables which they raised and grew themselves. Some families kept a cow for milk and cheese, raised chickens for eggs, and pigs for meat. When it was slaughtered, just before the winter, every part of the pig would have been eaten. The tongue would have been pickled, the ears and trotters used to flavour stews and soups, and the fat would have been spread on bread.

Many cottages were built on common land to avoid paying rent to a landowner. These were called squatters' cottages, and they often consisted of two small rooms, where families of seven or eight would live. The family would have gathered wood for fuel and made their own furniture. Clothes were handed down from one generation to the next. In the wintertime, the family would have gone to bed early so they didn't burn too many candles.

**In the kitchen of a squatters' cottage, a woman checks the stew cooking on the range.**

Bedroom    Stew pot

Hessian apron    Colander

Firewood    Iron

# Life in the Towns

Families that moved to industrial towns had mixed fortunes. Factory workers found they had money in their pockets, but they worked long hours to earn it. Often they lived in overcrowded streets in houses that had been built quickly on the doorsteps of factories. In Leeds, Manchester and other industrial cities, large families crammed into back-to-back houses with no toilets or running water. In cities like Glasgow, families lived in single rooms in large tenement blocks. Wherever working-class people lived, the air hung with smoke that billowed out of the factories. Children had nowhere to play except the dirty streets, which were filled with slops and piles of horse dung.

**By 7 a.m. in a Victorian street, people have already started their working day.**

Laundry woman    Pub landlord

Milk-delivery boy    Slops

14

**In a townhouse kitchen, a woman puts a kettle on the range.**

Inside a typical working-class family's townhouse, the cast-iron range was at the heart of the home. Its hot surfaces heated water for food and washing, and it had an oven in the centre. Stews and soups were often put in the oven in the morning so they would be ready at night. As dinner bubbled away in the oven, the washing was usually hung up to dry over the range. At night, families gathered in the kitchen to warm themselves around the dying embers. Some families couldn't afford a range, so they took their meals to a communal oven, or to the baker's to be cooked, instead.

Later in the nineteenth century, conditions in towns began to improve. Gas lighting was introduced, and shops, hospitals, churches, schools, public houses and music halls sprang up. Towns became places where people could better themselves. The educated or ambitious could take respectable, white-collar jobs in banking, insurance or education. They became the middle classes, and they looked for homes to reflect their new status. Hundreds of houses were built away from the industrial smog, on the outskirts of towns. Families living in the suburbs had bigger homes with gardens.

Range

Kettle

Washing

Bread

Iron and stand

Hot-water bottle

Clothes pegs

Frying pan

# Running the Home

A famous saying in Victorian times was 'a woman's place is in the home'. Most working-class women also had jobs working in factories, taking in laundry or looking after children. But they were still expected to do all the housework.

A typical day for most housewives included throwing out the slops, tidying the house, scrubbing the range, making sure the fire was kept alight, and mending clothes. Cleanliness was a sign of respectability, so the front step and even the pavement in front of each house were scrubbed. In some ways the weekly wash day must have been a welcome relief from the daily routine. Hanging out the washing in the back yard gave an opportunity to gossip with the neighbours over the fence.

**A woman scrubs the washing on the washboard.**

Range

Pan of hot water

Water pump

Washboard

Stone sink

Carpet beater

**A maid dusts the furniture of a middle-class home.**

By the 1880s, the most common job for women was domestic work. Middle-class families usually employed at least one servant to help the lady of the house. Servants had to work very hard. It was considered much better to get a job in a larger household, where there was a whole army of different servants to help do the work.

Cleaning was time-consuming because everything had to be done by hand. There were no vacuum cleaners so floors had to be swept, and rugs cleaned with tea-leaves and beaten with brushes. People used bars of carbolic soap or home-made mixtures of vinegar and bicarbonate of soda to clean their homes.

Most maids started work at 6 a.m. and, depending on their workload, went to bed at 11 p.m. They usually had a half day off on Sunday, one day off a month and two weeks' holiday a year.

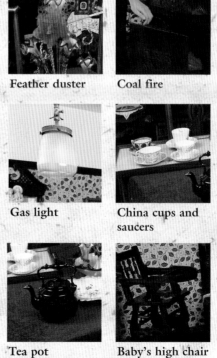

Feather duster

Coal fire

Gas light

China cups and saucers

Tea pot

Baby's high chair

# Keeping Clean

In Victorian times, people were not as clean as we are today. In the early nineteenth century, most people washed their hands, face and feet every day, and had a bath every Saturday, when the whole family would share the water. Homes that could afford running water were only supplied for a few hours a day. Everybody else had to collect water from taps and wells in the street. If they wanted hot water, they had to boil it on the range.

Later in the nineteenth century metal pipes were introduced, which connected more homes to the water supply. By the 1890s, most middle-class homes had bathrooms with hot running water and daily bathing became fashionable. A wide variety of toiletries became available and advertisements for sweet-smelling soaps and perfumed talcum powders regularly appeared in ladies' magazines.

**A man carefully shaves himself with a cut-throat razor.**

Jug of water     China basin

Soap     Shaving jug

Shaving brush     Using a cut-throat razor

**Tippler toilet**

**Newspaper**

Most people only used the outside toilet in the daytime. At night, it was usually too cold and dark, so they used chamber pots instead. Torn-up newspaper was used for toilet paper.

Sewerage was one of the biggest problems in Victorian towns. The open sewers not only smelt bad, they caused terrible diseases such as typhoid and cholera, which struck whole communities. Most working-class people had outdoor toilets, often shared with a whole row of houses. Tippler toilets had to be 'flushed out' with a bucket of water after being used. At night people used chamber pots, which they emptied each morning into open sewers, called cesspools. The cesspools had to be emptied regularly by 'night soil men'. In 1858, the Thames was so full of waste that an appalling stink rose up from the river and forced parliament to close.

By the middle of the nineteenth century, reformers had begun to look for ways of dealing with the sewage problem. In 1848, the Public Health Act stated that all new homes should have a toilet. The changes were slow, but in the following decades new types of flushing toilets were invented, and most cities established an underground network of sewers.

# Food Shopping

**A butcher weighs a few slices of black pudding for his customer.**

Victorian homes didn't have refrigerators, so people shopped for fresh produce every day. They visited small shops, such as bakers and butchers. A butcher would have had many types of meat that you don't see in supermarkets today. Game such as pheasants and hares were hung up on hooks. The butcher also stocked pig's bladders, which were blown up by children and used as footballs.

A typical poor Victorian family living in a town would have had about 12 shillings to spend on food each week. A quarter of this money would have been spent on bread alone. At that time, a loaf of bread cost about 3 pennies. The rest

Hare

Goose

Wood pigeons

Pheasants

Black pudding

Pig's bladder

Hanging scales

Cash register

Price in pence

would have been spent on milk, cheese, sugar, flour, dripping, meat, fish, potatoes and vegetables. Out of these ingredients, the family would have had one hot meal a day, and roast meat or a home-made pie on Sunday.

As towns got bigger, shops began to change. In some towns, chain-stores like Sainsbury's and the Co-op were first opened. As well as basics like bread and cheese, customers could now find exciting new ranges of tinned food. Some of the branded foods we eat today were introduced in Victorian times, including Heinz Baked Beans in 1875. Some food, such as flour, was not ready-packaged. It was scooped out of large sacks, weighed, and put in brown paper bags. People also relied on street traders, who sold anything from fruit and vegetables to poached game. In some areas people filled their jugs with milk from a churn, which was brought around by a milkman.

**Through the window of a general store, a shopkeeper scoops flour out of a sack on to the scales.**

Meat pies

Bovril

Rabbits

Tins

Flour sack

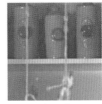
Stone bottles

# Disease and Medicine

Poison bottle

Medicine bottle

Pot of leeches

Poultice (mixture put on wounds)

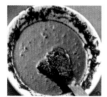
Herb mixture

Herbal remedy

Dried garlic

**A collection of herbal medicines.**

Throughout Victoria's reign, diseases like cholera, tuberculosis and typhoid were common. In 1848, a cholera epidemic wiped out 72,000 people. Poor sanitation and ignorance about how diseases were spread were the main causes. Another problem was the great divide between the rich and the poor. Doctors cost money and hospitals were often privately run. The poor couldn't afford medical treatment, so they visited chemists for advice instead.

If people couldn't afford to buy medicines, they used traditional herbal remedies or home-made cures. A mixture of vinegar and onions was regularly taken for coughs, and lard (pig fat) was smeared on the chest for colds. One of the most popular treatments for all kinds of illnesses was bloodletting. This involved live leeches being placed on the patient's body and allowed to suck their blood. In Victorian times thousands of strange medicines were invented, but they were rarely effective. One of the most important breakthroughs was the discovery of antiseptic to kill germs.

**(Right) A chemist makes pills by rolling the pill mixture into a long line and cutting it using the machine in front of him.**

# Getting Around

In busy towns, the sounds of hooves and turning wheels were part of everyday life, as were the tonnes of dung that made the streets smell like a stable-yard. The coming of the railways transformed Britain, but horses were always an important form of transport. The trusty horse carried people on its back, and pulled anything from cartloads of goods to stage-coaches filled with passengers. Large workhorses were generally used for pulling heavy loads or ploughing fields. Horses were expensive to buy and keep, so poorer people often bought ponies or donkeys to do their heavy work.

Workhorse          Cobbled street

Soap advert        Public house

**In towns, people got about on foot, or by horse and cart.**

To meet the demands of the industrial revolution, a network of artificial rivers, or canals, was built throughout Britain to move heavy goods around the country. Between the 1760s and the 1830s, over 6,400 km of canals were built. The first canal boats were pulled by men with ropes from the canal banks. Later, when it was discovered that horses could do the job better, towpaths were built alongside the canals. One large horse could pull a boat weighing 30 tonnes. Where the canals went through tunnels, the towpaths went around the side and men had to take over by legging the boats through the tunnels. By the late nineteenth century there were a few steam-powered boats, but it wasn't until diesel boats were introduced in 1911 that men could finally leave the hard work to an engine.

**A boatman legs his narrowboat through a tunnel.**

# The Railway Age

In the early nineteenth century, Britain relied on its waterways for carrying its heavy goods but by the 1830s, trains were starting to take over. Trains were faster, more economical, and could carry more goods than narrow canal boats.

Trains opened up long-distance travel to the public, too. The first passenger railway was opened in 1825 between Stockton and Darlington. A chain of carriages was pulled along by a steam locomotive designed by George Stephenson. In 1830, the Liverpool-to-Manchester line was opened. Once again, one of Stephenson's locomotives was leading the way. It travelled at an average speed of 12 miles per hour, which was quicker than any other form of transport. Very soon, the train replaced the stage-coach for carrying passengers over long distances.

Most Victorians fell in love with the railway because it made it possible to visit places in a number of hours that had taken days to get to by road. By the end of the nineteenth century, the railway network stretched the length and breadth of Britain, and the fastest trains were averaging speeds of 55 miles per hour. Each service had first, second and third-class carriages, so everyone could afford to travel. On bank holidays and during the summer, the railway stations were jammed with people going on day-trips or holidays to the coast.

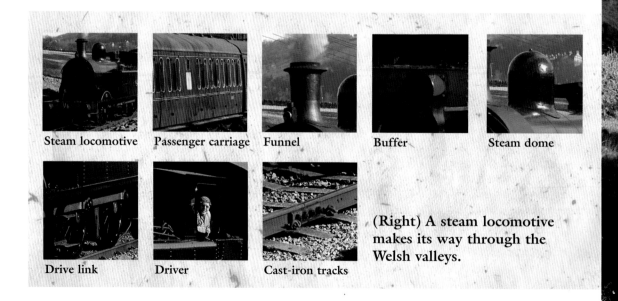

Steam locomotive    Passenger carriage    Funnel    Buffer    Steam dome

Drive link    Driver    Cast-iron tracks

(Right) A steam locomotive makes its way through the Welsh valleys.

# Timeline

**1819**
24 May   Princess Victoria is born.

**1825**   The first public railway is opened from Darlington to Stockton.

**1837**   King William IV dies. Victoria becomes Queen of England.

**1838**   Queen Victoria's coronation. Louis Daguerre develops photography in France. First steamboat crossing of the Atlantic.

**1840**
Feb   Queen Victoria marries Prince Albert.

**1841**   Thomas Cook introduces railway excursions.

**1844**   The First Factory Act restricts the working day to 12 hours for women and 6 hours for children aged between 8 and 13.

**1847**   The Second Factory Act restricts the working day to 10 hours for women and children.

**1848**   Public Health Act aims to make towns cleaner and healthier.

**1849**   A cholera epidemic in London kills 14,000 people.

**1854–6**   Crimean War fought by Britain and France against Russia.

**1861**   Prince Albert dies from typhoid.

**1862**   The world's first underground railway is opened in London.

**1864**   Boys under the age of 10 are banned from climbing inside chimneys to clean them.

**1865**   Sir Joseph Bazalgette builds the first underground London sewers.

**1867**   The Third Factory Act reduces the working day to ten hours for everyone.

**1867 continued**

Dr Barnado opens a children's shelter in Stepney, London. Joseph Lister discovers antiseptic surgery.

**1870**   The Elementary Education Act (Forster's Act) makes elementary education available to every child.

**1877**   Queen Victoria is proclaimed Empress of India.

**1878**   The first electric street lights are turned on in London.

**1879**   The cash register is invented in the USA.

**1880**   The Education Act makes schooling compulsory for children aged between 5 and 13.

**1886**   Coca-Cola is first manufactured in the USA.

**1887**   Queen Victoria celebrates her Golden Jubilee (50 years as queen).

**1890**   The first underground electric railway is opened in London.

**1895**   The first motorcar factory is opened in Birmingham.

**1897**   Queen Victoria celebrates her Diamond Jubilee (60 years as queen).

**1898**   Cornflakes are first manufactured in the USA.

**1899
–1902**   The Boer War is fought between Britain and the Boers in South Africa.

**1900**   The Mines Act is passed, which makes it illegal for children under the age of 13 to work in the pits.

**1901**
22 Jan   Queen Victoria dies aged 81. Her eldest son, Edward VII, becomes King of England.

# Glossary

**antiseptic** A substance that kills germs and prevents the spread of infection.

**apprentice** A person who learns a trade by being employed in it for an agreed period of time at a low wage.

**birth control** The methods used to prevent a woman becoming pregnant. Also known as contraception.

**black pudding** A kind of sausage made from pork and dried pig's blood.

**carbolic soap** A strong-smelling soap which acts as a disinfectant.

**cesspool** An underground pool where human waste, or sewage, is temporarily stored.

**chamber pots** A portable pottery container for urinating in.

**cholera** A dangerous infectious disease, carried in dirty water, which causes sickness and diarrhoea, and sometimes death.

**churn** A large metal container for milk.

**class** A group of people in society with similar backgrounds.

**common land** Land that belongs to the whole community.

**domestic work** A job looking after somebody else's home.

**dormitory** A big bedroom shared by a large number of people.

**dripping** Fat collected from boiled or roasted beef which can be used again for cooking or eating.

**foundlings** Children who have been abandoned by their parents.

**locomotive** A steam-powered railway engine.

**mass-produced** Made in large quantities, usually by machines in factories.

**oakum** Loose fibre obtained by picking apart old rope.

**sanitation** A system of keeping places clean and protecting people from diseases, for example, by providing a clean water supply and a sewage system.

**shillings** Coins used in Britain before 1971. There were 12 pence in one shilling.

**slops** Waste liquid and dirty water from the kitchen and bathroom.

**smog** A mixture of fog and smoke.

**social campaigners** People who speak out against bad working and living conditions and try to make the government change the laws to make conditions better for everybody.

**squatter** A person who lives on empty land or property without the permission of the owner.

**terraced housing** A row of houses joined together.

**tuberculosis** A serious infectious disease which killed millions of European people during the nineteenth century.

**typhoid** A serious infectious disease that causes sickness, diarrhoea, fever, and sometimes death. It is caused by germs in water or food.

**white-collar jobs** Jobs that are based in an office.

**workhouses** Institutions for poor people where they did unpaid work in return for food and shelter.

# Activities

## pp4–5 Who Were the Victorians?
- Ask your parents if there are any old family photographs from Victorian times, or look for photographs of Victorian families in books. Compare them with photographs of your family today.
- Write a letter to a Victorian child, asking them what you'd like to know about their everyday life. Describe the things you can do in the twenty-first century that they could not do in the nineteenth century. Ask a member of your class to write back as if they were the Victorian child.

## pp6–7 The Industrial Revolution
- Write a newspaper report about a terrible coal-mining disaster. If you live in an old coal-mining region, look at newspapers in your local library to find out about accidents that happened in your area.
- Look at the census for your area in your local library. Find a census for between 1841 and 1891. What was the main occupation in your area? How has it changed today?

## pp8–9 The Changing Workplace
- Interview your local shoe-repairer to find out what has changed since being a shoemaker in Victorian times. Compare the equipment he or she uses today with the equipment in the photo on page 8.
- Design a poster for the print shop on page 9 to make. It could be an advertisement for a job, or for goods.

## pp10–11 Child Labour
- Imagine what it was like for a poor child working in a coal mine. Write a diary entry about a typical day, starting when you got out of bed.

- Write a short play about a group of child apprentices who are planning to run away from their apprentice house.

## pp12–13 Life in the Countryside
- Write a timetable for a day in the life of a squatter family. Include jobs such as feeding the pigs, gathering firewood, tending the vegetable patch, cooking and cleaning.
- Draw a plan of the house on page 13. Label the position of the range, beds for six children and two adults, a table and chairs.

## pp14–15 Life in the Towns
- Compare the street where you live with the street in the photo. Look at the buildings, the pavement and the jobs people are doing. What are the similarities and differences from your street?
- Look at the housing in your area and find out when it was built. Was it built for working-class or middle-class people? If you live in a Victorian house, think about how it has changed since it was built.

## pp16–17 Running the Home
- Write a diary for a day in the life of a working-class Victorian housewife. Include jobs such as throwing out the slops, washing and mending clothes.
- Imagine you are the wealthy owner of a Victorian house. Write a list of instructions for your maid telling her the jobs she needs to do in the next week.

## pp18–19 Keeping Clean
- Hunt through old Victorian magazines for advertisements for toiletries. Design your own advertisement for a new product.
- Write a newspaper report with a shocking headline about the 'Great Stink' in London in 1858.

### pp20–21 Food Shopping

- Write a shopping list for a poor family of ten in about 1900. Remember you don't have a fridge, so don't buy anything that won't keep. Include the shops you will visit for each type of food.
- What kind of shops are in your local area? Were any of them built in Victorian times? How have they changed since that time?

### pp22–23 Disease and Medicine

- Visit your local library and use the microfilm to look at local newspapers from Victorian times. Look at the advertisements for health products and medicines. Make up your own advertisement for a new kind of health product.
- Ask your local chemist how pills are made today. Compare it with the way the chemist is making pills in the photo on page 23.

### pp24–25 Getting Around

- Imagine you are a time-traveller who has been transported back in time to a Victorian town for a day. Write a tourist guide about the sights and sounds of the city.
- Look at maps of your local area and find out if any canals were built near you. Are they still in existence? Do people still use them today?

### pp26–27 The Railway Age

- Design a poster for a Victorian railway station advertising day trips or holidays at the seaside.
- Write a story about a school day trip to the seaside in Victorian times. Discuss things like what the railway station was like, what it felt like to be on board a train and how fast the train went.

# Finding Out More

**Books to Read**

*All About the Industrial Revolution* by Peter Hepplewhite and Mairi Campbell (Hodder Wayland, 2002)

*All About the Victorians* by Jane Goodwin (Hodder Wayland, 2001)

*Digital Time Traveller: The Real Victorians* (TAG Publishing, 2003)

*Heritage: The Victorians* by Robert Hull (Hodder Children's Books, 2000)

*The Illustrated World of The Victorians* by Richard Wood and Sara Wood (Hodder Wayland, 2001)

*In Their Own Words: The Victorians* by Robert Hull (Watts, 2001)

*The Past in Pictures: The Victorians* by John Malam (Hodder Wayland, 2002)

**Places to Visit**

The Boat Museum, South Pier Road, Ellesmere Port, Cheshire CH65 4FW
The photograph of the man legging through a tunnel was taken at this museum, which houses boats and equipment used in Victorian times.

The Black Country Living Museum, Tipton Road, Dudley, West Midlands DY1 4SQ
Many of the photographs that appear in this book, including the street scenes, the chemist's shop and the Victorian kitchen were taken at this museum.

Blists Hill Victorian Town, Legge Way, Madeley, Telford, Shropshire TF7 5DY
The squatter's cottage, the cobbler's shop and the butcher's shop are all part of this recreation of a late-Victorian working town.

# Index

Page numbers in **bold** refer to photographs.

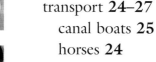